NIST

**National Institute of
Standards and Technology**

U.S. Department of Commerce

NIST IR-7658

Guide to SIMfill Use and Development

Wayne Jansen
Aurélien Delaitre

NIST IR-7658

Guide to SIMfill Use and Development
Wayne Jansen
Aurélien Delaitre

C O M P U T E R   S E C U R I T Y

Computer Security Division
Information Technology Laboratory
National Institute of Standards and Technology
Gaithersburg, MD 20899-8930

February 2010

U.S. Department of Commerce
Gary Locke, Secretary

National Institute of Standards and Technology
Patrick D. Gallagher, Director

Reports on Computer Systems Technology

The Information Technology Laboratory (ITL) at the National Institute of Standards and Technology (NIST) promotes the U.S. economy and public welfare by providing technical leadership for the Nation's measurement and standards infrastructure. ITL develops tests, test methods, reference data, proof of concept implementations, and technical analysis to advance the development and productive use of information technology. ITL's responsibilities include the development of technical, physical, administrative, and management standards and guidelines for the cost-effective security and privacy of sensitive unclassified information in Federal computer systems. This Interagency Report discusses ITL's research, guidance, and outreach efforts in computer security, and its collaborative activities with industry, government, and academic organizations.

National Institute of Standards and Technology Interagency Report
58 pages (2010)

Abstract

SIMfill is a proof-of-concept, open source, application developed by NIST to populate identity modules with test data, as a way to assess the recovery capability of mobile forensic tools. An initial set of test data is also provided with SIMfill as a baseline for creating other test cases. This report describes the design and organization of SIMfill in sufficient detail to allow informed use and experimentation with the software and test data provided, including the option to modify and extend the program and data provided to meet specific needs.

Keywords: *Computer Forensics; Reference Materials; Tool Validation*

Table of Contents

1. Introduction

Reference materials are vital in forensic laboratories and similar settings, where quality assurance is a major issue. Reference material refers to material, sufficiently homogeneous and stable with respect to one or more specified properties, which has been established to be fit for its intended use in a measurement process. One area of application is in the validation of forensic tools to identify inaccuracies that might exist and establish overall suitability for use. New versions of forensic software tools are issued regularly by a tool manufacturer to broaden the range of existing functions, provide new features, and correct identified problems. After the laboratory successfully validates a tool, it can be safely put into use for its intended purpose.

Reference materials, such as handsets and identity modules containing populated data, are typically used to validate forensic tools targeting mobile handheld devices. However, populating such devices with data that exhibit the needed properties, including a broad range of character sets, data structures, and file content, is difficult. Populating a device with a representative data to create suitable reference material can be done in various ways:

- Manually – Using manual means to populate a group of individual items onto devices is typically a time-consuming and error-prone process, since it is normally done through the user interface of a handset.

- Semi-automated – Using a semi-automated process typically preserves manually populated data for reuse by copying or transferring the data to another device with the same or very similar characteristics.

- Automated – Using an automated means to populate devices through a well-defined interface can greatly expedite validation, once the initial effort to construct the test data is completed.

SIMfill is a proof-of-concept application developed to expedite validation by populating certain devices automatically with test data, to create reference material for tool assessment.[1] SIMfill works with Subscriber Identity Modules (SIMs) found in many present-day mobile phones. Universal Mobile Telecommunications System (UMTS) SIMs (USIMs) being deployed in 3G networks are often backwards-compatible with SIMs and able to be populated by SIMfill as well [3GPP09c]. (U)SIMs are highly standardized devices with well-defined interfaces. The vast majority of forensic tools for cell phones provides the functionality to recover (U)SIM-resident data, making SIMfill a potentially useful means for use in assessing their capabilities.

This report describes the design and organization of SIMfill in sufficient detail to allow informed use and experimentation with the software distribution, including the option to modify the program and test dataset provided to meet specific needs. The reader is presumed to have a fundamental understanding of the SIM file system (e.g., see [3GPP07,

---

[1] The reference material described in this report is not to be confused with NIST Standard Reference Materials - http://ts.nist.gov/measurementservices/referencematerials/index.cfm.

Jan09]). The reader is advised to review the disclaimer file included in the distribution before attempting to use SIMfill or any of its components.

2. Overview

SIMfill is open source software written in the Java programming language. It was developed using Eclipse 3.2.1 on Windows XP SP3 and uses the Jaccal library to communicate with the (U)SIM card. Jaccal is compliant with the Personal Computer/Smart Card (PC/SC) interface specifications and is also open source.

Two different types of input data are needed for SIMfill to perform its tasks, as illustrated in Figure 1:

- A data file containing the test cases to be written to the Elementary Files (EFs) of interest in the SIM file system.

- A card file containing any codes needed to satisfy the various access conditions of a target (U)SIM and establish the access required to populate EFs of interest.

The baseline test data and card data provided with SIMfill are represented as Extensible Markup Language (XML) files. XML schema definition files are also provided that specify in detail how the input data are to be represented. The choice of XML representation allows the input to be easily modified by users to suit their needs using a freely available XML editor, such as Microsoft's XML Notepad.

The test data and card data must be both well-formed and valid XML documents. The former means that the syntax meets the XML standard, while latter means that the well-formed content also conforms to the XML schema definitions provided. By definition, all XML editors perform syntax checks. Many of them also perform XML schema validation dynamically during editing, which greatly simplifies the task of preparing conforming documents. SIMfill also checks the card and data files during execution.

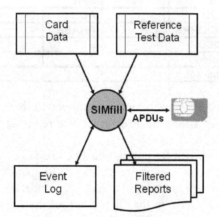

Figure 1: SIMfill Overview

The dataset provided with SIMfill can be used to get started. Note that the data content to be populated is kept separate from device programming commands. Instead, populating an identity module is data driven, guided entirely by the reference test data specified and done in accordance with the established access conditions.

During the population process, SIMfill makes detailed entries to an event log, including the Application Protocol Data Units (APDUs) exchanged and success or failure of the operation, as shown in Figure 1. Various levels of filtering can be selected for the entries in the event log to allow the contents of the log to be viewed at different levels of detail and captured as a report.

Table 1 list the abbreviations for EFs that are used in the Global System for Mobile Communications (GSM) specifications [e.g., 3GPP07, 3GPP09a, 3GPP09b] and are able to be specified by name in the reference test data. The required access conditions needed to write to an EF given in the body of the table are listed across the top of the table:

- Card Holder Verification 1 (CHV1) - Update can be performed only after a successful verification of the user's PIN, or if PIN verification is disabled

- Card Holder Verification 2 (CHV2) - Update can be performed only after a successful verification of the user's PIN2, or if PIN2 verification is disabled

- Administrative (ADM) - Update can be performed only after prescribed requirements for administrative access are fulfilled

- Never - Access of the file over the SIM interface to the handset is forbidden.[2]

Table 1: Elementary Files Populated by SIMfill

CHV1	CHV2	ADM	NEVER
ADN	FDN	IMSI	ICCID
EXT1	EXT2	SDN	
LND		EXT3	
SMS		SPN	
LOCI		AD	
LOCIGPRS		PHASE	
MSISDN		SST	
FPLMN			
PLMNsel			

In addition to these named EFs, a generic EF is supported that can be used to identify and populate the contents of any file in the directory structure, using its16-bit file identifier.

A common alternative to SIMfill for populating a (U)SIM is to use an editor tool designed specifically for smart cards or identity modules. Commands normally follow a simple format with keywords and parameters that the tool understands to perform associated activities, such as locating an EF in the file system of the module and writing data to it. The commands are translated into APDUs that are used to communicate with the identity module to carry out a function.

---

[2] Note that with some developer identity modules, it is possible to update the ICCID, contrary to the standardized access condition for that EF.

Such editor tools often allow several commands to be linked together in a script and executed, using additional commands used to control the flow of execution. For example, if a referenced EF does not exist or a command fails for some other reason, the flow of control needs to be programmed to catch such conditions and debugged, much like a programming language. Gaining expertise with a new command language and preparing scripts is a drawback with this approach. Another drawback is the representation of data; typically the data to be populated is embedded within the script, making creation and update problematic.

3. Installation and Operation

Installing SIMfill is fairly straightforward. The SIMfill distribution package can be found at http://csrc.nist.gov/groups/SNS/mobile_security/mobile_forensics_software.html. Download and unzip the file on the target computer. Please note the disclaimer for the distribution. Then, download and install the java runtime needed for SIMfill to execute, if it is not already installed. The java runtime can be found at http://www.java.com/en/download/index.jsp.

Jaccal, which is used to communicate with a smart card, is available from the sourceforge Web site at http://jaccal.sourceforge.net/. The Win32 binary release contains a collection of files, including Windows executables, Java Archive (jar) files and a Windows dynamic-link library (dll) file. Only the jaccal-core.jar and jaccal-pcsc.dll files from the Jaccal release package are required for SIMfill to function. Copy the jaccal-core.jar file to the same directory as the simfill-1.2.jar file. Also, copy the jaccal-pcsc.dll file to c:\windows\system32 or other system-path accessible dll directory. Since Jaccal works with a PC/SC-compatible smart card reader, one of them also must also be installed.

At this stage installation is finished. To execute SIMfill, simply navigate to the simfill.jar file and double click it.

3.1 User Interface

When SIMfill begins execution, it presents the user with a very simple interface illustrated in Figure 2. Its main functions are represented by three buttons across the top of the user interface.

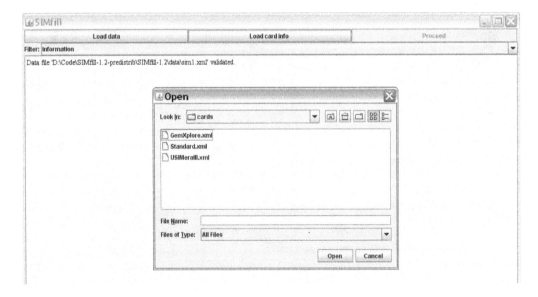

Figure 2: SIMfill User Interface

The two active buttons shown, labeled Load data, Load card info, allow the user to select and load the test data file to populate and the card information for the target (U)SIM to be populated. As selections are made, entries appear in the filtered event log window at the bottom of the user interface. During loading, the files are validated against their respective schema definitions and any errors are logged. In the Figure 2 example, the data file has been successfully loaded and validated, and the card information file is about to be selected.

The population of the (U)SIM cannot begin until both files are successfully loaded and validated. Once that occurs, the third button, labeled Proceed, is activated to allow the population process to be initiated upon its selection. It is important to insert (U)SIM into the smart card reader before initiating the population process. Otherwise an error occurs immediately. Population of the (U)SIM should then proceed automatically through to completion and continue to fill the event log window with event entries.

Note that six levels of filtering are available to allow viewing of log entries at an appropriate level of detail, including a full listing of each APDU exchanged with the (U)SIM. The choice of filtering level is selectable via a pull-down menu, as illustrated in Figure 3. For speedier processing, it is recommended that detailed views of the event log (i.e., Report, Debug, and All) remain off until processing is completed. All log information is captured regardless of the filtering level, but displaying the details more fully during processing incurs delay. The filtering level can be changed to a more detailed view, once processing is completed, and the information captured for a report.

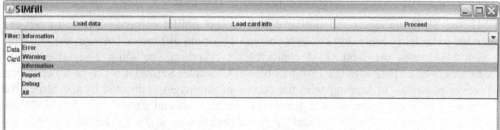

Figure 3: Filtering Level Selection

When SIMfill completes processing it posts a notification in the event log and deactivates the button labeled Proceed. At the bottom of the user interface, two buttons labeled Clear and Save are activated. Typically the user selects a filtering level and reviews the events displayed. If satisfied with the results, the Save button can be used to capture the events as a report file for later use in the assessment process; otherwise, the Clear button can be used to empty the event log for another attempt, once corrections to the dataset are done.

3.2 Reference Data

The baseline reference data provided in the SIMfill distribution contains several predefined card information and test data files as a starting point. Three card files are included: GemXplore.xml, USIMeraIII.xml, and Standard.xml. They are shown in the pop-up menu in Figure 2. The GemXplorer.xml and USIMeraIII.xml are associated with specific developer SIMs, which can be used to enable ADM access, as well as CHV1 and CHV2 access, and provide the means to specify the broadest range of possible test cases, including all EFs listed in Table 1.[3] They serve mainly as a model for preparing card files for other developer SIMs. Standard.xml is for use with common SIMs issued by cellular carriers. The file can be used to supply CHV1 and CHV2 values and gain access, if those settings are enabled.

The reference test data includes three XML files, each containing data to populate a single (U)SIM. They are referred to as SIM1, SIM2, and SIM3. The SIM1.xml and SIM2.xml files contain the basic reference data cases, while SIM3.xml contains unconventional data cases used primarily for experimentation. Figure 4 illustrates the situation.

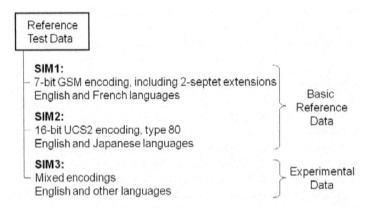

Figure 4: Reference Test Data

SIM1 and SIM2 are structured similarly and contain similar content. The test cases are intended to be fairly basic, but comprehensive. The main difference between the two files is that SIM1 uses the 7-bit GSM character set encoding, including 2-septet extended characters, while SIM2 uses the 16-bit Universal Character Set 2 (UCS2) type 80 encoding wherever possible. In keeping with the choice of languages supported by the respective character sets, the languages used for SIM1 are English and French and for SIM2 are English and Japanese. SIM1 encodes language preferences in the LP EF, and SIM2 uses the ELP EF. Both single segment and long multi-segment concatenated Short Message Service (SMS) messages are included in the reference data as well as Enhanced Message Service (EMS) messages containing black and white graphics. Appendix B illustrates the SIM1 and SIM2 data entries for ADN and SMS EFs, highlighting the similarities and characteristics of the content.

SIM3 contains both 7-bit GSM and 16-bit UCS2 character sets. The data cases are more uncommon or unusual and some can be considered to be of an anti-forensic nature. Examples of the former include concatenated messages comprising more than four segments and ADN entries with an alpha-identifier encoded entirely in 7-bit GSM

---

[3] The GemXplore xml file is provided for Gemplus GemXplore 3G identity modules, and the USIMeraIII.xml file for Axalto SIMagination (USIMERA Classic 3) identity modules, both of which are now out of production.

extended characters. Examples of the latter include LND entries with a circularly linked EXT1 extension chain, which can throw some forensic tools into an indefinite loop.

3.3 Population Process

SIMfill populates a (U)SIM on an EF by EF basis in the order data appears in the test data file. It uses the codes (e.g., PIN1 and PIN2) given in the card data file to satisfy the access condition of the EFs and gain the ability to write to them. Before an EF gets populated, SIMfill erases its contents completely. Generally this means that all bits in the file are set to 1. Exceptions may exist, however. For example, the flag for SMS entries containing "free space" must instead be set to zero.

SIMfill attempts to erase and process only those EFs specified in the test data file. All other EFs are ignored. If sufficient access to update an EF is not granted either through the access codes specified in the card file or the settings of the identity module, an error occurs. SIMfill reports the error and continues with the next EF specified. Because the characteristics of identity modules can vary, in particular the length of a field or number of records in a linear fixed file, test data may sometimes exceed those limits. To accommodate such situations, data written to a shorter field is truncated and excess records are dropped. SIMfill logs such events as a warning message for the user.

The implications of the procedure used by SIMfill are important to understand when using or modifying the baseline test data provided, or creating new test data. The process allows the freedom to experiment with simple test data cases, involving only a single EF, while not affecting other EFs on a (U)SIM. However, any EF intended to be empty (i.e., erased and not populated with any test data) must be specified explicitly in the data file as a null entry. Otherwise, the content remains unchanged. Similarly, one must be aware of the field length and record number limits of (U)SIMs being populated when constructing test data. If not careful, important parts of a test case could be truncated or dropped.

4. Data and Schema Definitions

The choice of XML as a representation for the data used by SIMfill has several advantages. XML is a well-known and well-defined standard, similar to the Hypertext Markup Language (HTML). Most users are likely to be familiar with it or with HTML, which lessens the learning curve. XML scheme definitions can also be specified for a document to exert control over its contents. Schema-sensitive XML editors are widely available, and many of them are free. With such an editor, it is fairly easy to modify existing or create new reference test data conforming to the schema definition.

Changes to the XML schema definitions provided in the SIMfill distribution normally are not needed unless an error is discovered or the capabilities of SIMfill are modified to accommodate additional EFs or other types of identity modules. Nevertheless, some basic understanding is helpful, particularly if using an XML editor to modify or create test data.

Two schema definition files are provided in the SIMfill distribution: one for the test data and the other for the card information. They are respectively called data.xsd and card.xsd. Schema definition files are in and of themselves XML files. The schema definition files are used to define a set of elements, their attributes, and their relationship to one another. In the case of data.xsd, the schema elements closely reflect the elements in the GSM standards for the SIM file system [3GPP07, 3GPP09a, 3GPP09b, 3GPP07b]. Therefore, familiarity with the GSM standards simplifies reading the schema definition and the data represented using it.

To illustrate the relationship between the standard definition of an EF, its XML scheme definition, and the encoding of test data for the EF, the Abbreviated Dialing Numbers (ADN) is used as an example. ADN entries essentially provide a phonebook of numbers and identifiers for the user and are a valuable source of data for an investigator. While conceptually simple, the encodings used and supplemental information can be quite detailed.

4.1 Standard EF Definition

Figure 5 is a simplified excerpt taken from the GSM standard defining the contents of the ADN EF [3GPP07].

Identifier: '6F3A'		Structure: linear fixed	
Record length: X+14 bytes		Update access condition: CHV1	
Bytes	**Description**		**Length**
1 to X	Alpha Identifier		X bytes
X+1	Length of BCD number		1 byte
X+2	TON and NPI		1 byte
X+3 to X+12	Dialing Number		10 bytes
X+13	Capability/Configuration Identifier		1 byte
X+14	Extension1 Record Identifier		1 byte

Figure 5: ADN EF Record Description

In this definition, the length of each record in the linear fixed file is X+14 bytes, where X is the number of bytes in the Alpha Identifier (i.e., a descriptor) for the Dialing Number and may range from 0 to 241. The Alpha Identifier can be encoded using either one of the UCS2 encoding options, or the GSM default 7-bit coded alphabet with bit 8 set to 0, left justified, and unused bytes set to FF.

The Dialing Number has 10 bytes allocated for it, leaving the remaining 4 bytes of the record for attributes and identifiers associated with the Dialing Number.

The Length of Binary Coded Decimal (BCD) number/ Supplementary Service Control strings (SSC) contents indicates the number of bytes used for the data item containing the actual BCD number or SSC information.

The type of number (TON) and numbering plan identification (NPI) follow and are encoded in one byte as shown in Figure 6.

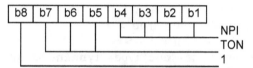

Figure 6: TON and NPI Representation in Byte X+2

The Dialing Number/SSC String contains up to 20 digits of the phone number or SSC information, encoded using 4-bit extended BCD. The ordering of the first two BCD digits is illustrated in Figure 7, including the least and most significant (i.e., LSB and MSB) layout. The pattern continues for additional digits. If the phone number or SSC is longer than 20 digits, only the first 20 digits are stored in this field; the remainder are stored in an associated record in the EXT1 EF and its index is placed the Extension1 Record Identifier field. Unused digits are set to F, for ADN/SSC numbers with less than 20 digits.

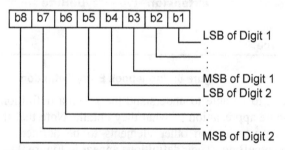

Figure 7: Dialing Number Representation in Bytes X+3 to X+12

The Capability/Configuration Identifier identifies the number of a record in the CCP EF, which contains capability/configuration parameters required for the call. This field is optional and set to FF, if unused.

4.2 XML Schema Definition

The XML schema definition for a phonebook entry is shown in Figure 8. It specifies the main elements of the record that makes up the Abbreviated Dialing Numbers (ADN) EF

11

(i.e., a contact list or phonebook): the description (i.e., Alpha Identifier), number (i.e., a Dialing Number, including Type of Number (TON) and Numbering Plan Identifier (NPI) designators), and two optional identifiers (i.e., Capability/Configuration Identifier and Extension1 Record Identifier). SIMfill computes the length of these items for the user.

The definition uses the XML schema elements defined by the World Wide Web Consortium's (W3C) XML Schema namespace and denoted with the "xs" prefix. The schema elements appearing in Figure 8 are identifiable as red characters. The name of the phonebook entry definition is typeContact. It is defined as a complex type consisting of a sequence of four other elements: description, address, capability, and extension.

```xml
<!-- Phonebook entry -->
<xs:complexType name="typeContact">
  <xs:sequence>

    <!-- Description of the contact -->
    <xs:element name="description">
      <xs:complexType mixed="true">
        <!-- Encoding of the name -->
        <xs:attribute name="enc" type="typeEncoding" />
      </xs:complexType>
    </xs:element>

    <!-- Address of the contact, i.e. the phone number, including TON and NPI -->
    <xs:element name="address" type="typeAddress" />

    <!-- Capability/configuration identifier - optional -->
    <xs:element name="capability" type="typeByte" minOccurs="0" />

    <!-- Extension record identifier - optional -->
    <xs:element name="extension" type="typeByte" minOccurs="0" />

  </xs:sequence>
</xs:complexType>
```

Figure 8: Phonebook Entry Definition

It is not important to be able to understand the schema definitions fully. However, it is useful to gain some appreciation of what they entail. Note that the schema definition for the phonebook entry relies on other elements to be defined, including typeEncoding, typeAddress, and typeByte. Their definitions appear in Figure 9.

```xml
<!-- Type describing the encoding used in various text fields, including contact names -->
<xs:simpleType name="typeEncoding">
  <xs:restriction base="xs:string">
    <xs:enumeration value="default" />
    <xs:enumeration value="ucs2" />
  </xs:restriction>
</xs:simpleType>
```

12

```xml
<!-- Type describing the address of a subscriber, i.e. the phone number  -->
<xs:complexType name="typeAddress">
  <xs:sequence>

    <!-- Type of number  -->
    <xs:element name="ton">
      <xs:simpleType>
        <xs:restriction base="xs:string">
          <xs:enumeration value="unknown" />
          <xs:enumeration value="international" />
          <xs:enumeration value="national" />
          <xs:enumeration value="network specific" />
          <xs:enumeration value="subscriber" />
          <xs:enumeration value="alphanumeric" />
          <xs:enumeration value="abbreviated" />
          <xs:enumeration value="reserved" />
        </xs:restriction>
      </xs:simpleType>
    </xs:element>

    <!-- Number plan identifier  -->
    <xs:element name="npi">
      <xs:simpleType>
        <xs:restriction base="xs:string">
          <xs:enumeration value="unknown" />
          <xs:enumeration value="telephone" />
          <xs:enumeration value="data" />
          <xs:enumeration value="telex" />
          <xs:enumeration value="service center specific 1" />
          <xs:enumeration value="service center specific 2" />
          <xs:enumeration value="national" />
          <xs:enumeration value="private" />
          <xs:enumeration value="ermes" />
          <xs:enumeration value="reserved" />
        </xs:restriction>
      </xs:simpleType>
    </xs:element>

<!-- Type describing a decimal number between 0 and 255  -->
<xs:simpleType name="typeByte">
  <xs:restriction base="xs:integer">
    <xs:minInclusive value="0" />
    <xs:maxInclusive value="255" />
  </xs:restriction>
</xs:simpleType>
```

Figure 9: Definitions of Supporting Elements

The schema definition can be quite detailed, as seen from these excerpts. Note, for example, how all the possible values for the TON and NPI are explicitly enumerated. This level of detail allows any corresponding document to be validated accordingly. Note too that the character set for text strings defaults to 7-bit GSM, for the typeEncoding element.

4.3 XML Data Representation

Once the schema is defined, using it to represent actual content is relatively straightforward by comparison. Figure 10 illustrates an instance of a basic phonebook entry (i.e., contact). The description containing the name "John Smith" is to be encoded using UCS2, which SIMfill does automatically for the user. Similarly the TON and NPI choices are encoded into a single byte, as indicated in Figure 6, and the digits of the 10-digit number are encoded using extended BCD, as indicated in Figure 7.

Appendix A gives an extensive list of examples for other elements that can be used to populate a (U)SIM.

```
<!-- Example entry with a 10-digit number -->
<contact>
   <description enc="ucs2">John Smith</description>
   <address>
     <ton>national</ton>
     <npi>telephone</npi>
     <number>3019758000</number>
   </address>
</contact>
```

Figure 10: Example Phonebook Entry

Using the phonebook entry in Figure 10 as a template, it should be easy for most readers to define additional entries that contain the same four elements of information. Figure 11 illustrates an example of another instance of contact entry for an individual in France. Note that accented characters and other special characters can appear in the description.

```
<!-- Additional entry with a 10-digit number -->
<contact>
   <description enc="ucs2">Clément [cell]</description>
   <address>
     <ton>international</ton>
     <npi>telephone</npi>
     <number>33139148000</number>
   </address>
</contact>
```

Figure 11: Additional Phonebook Entry Example

The full schema definition for the ADN EF allows an empty entry to be specified as an alternate to a contact entry. It is represented as `<empty/>`. Empty entries are defined for most linear fixed files, such as ADN, which are used to hold a list of records that are accessible individually. When SIMfill populates linear fixed files, it takes the first XML

14

element encountered and associates it with the first record slot in the EF. If the element is an empty entry, the record is skipped; otherwise, the data specified in the entry is written to the record.

The actual content to employ when creating test cases can come from a variety of sources, including previously acquired data that caused problems for some forensic tools and existing manually generated test cases used to assess tools. Despite the constraints imposed by the schema definition, for some elements, it is possible to specify content that is inconsistent with the content specified for other related elements and with the GSM standards. While SIMfill does restrict input to standard values, generally it is important to specify data that overall is self-consistent and can occur in practice. The one exception that may apply is testing the resiliency of forensic tools to handle anti-forensic data. That is, some (U)SIM EFs, such as those for phonebook entries and SMS messages, are under control of the user and may pose problems, if the contents have been manipulated to thwart recovery by a forensic tool [Jan09]. A generic EF called RAW allows considerable freedom in populating data, including anti-forensic data, and is discussed further in Appendix A.

5. Design and Implementation

SIMfill incorporates the Model-View-Controller (MVC) paradigm in its design. The view renders the content of the model in the user interface. The user interacts with a graphical user interface (GUI). The controller handles events from the view and notifies the model of the user action. The model embodies the behavior and the data of the application, responding to inquiries for data and to requests that affect the data.

SIMfill's structure employs two controllers for two respective models: the MainModel and the LogModel. The main model characterizes the reference data and (U)SIM population logic, while the log model characterizes the log events and filtering. A controller and its associated model form a distinct subsystem. The software is event-driven, carrying out operations only in reaction to user actions on the user interface, which are handled by the controllers. The view renders the data represented in these two models and receives notifications from them when their contents change. Figure 12 illustrates the overall organization.

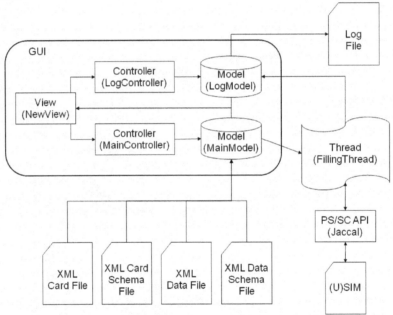

Figure 12: Model-View-Controller Components

The main method for SIMfill begins by initializing the registry, followed by the logging sub-system and the main sub-system, and finally the user interface. When the user interface is up and running, the program switches inherently from sequential to event-driven.

When the user selects the Load data button on the user interface, shown in Figure 2, the MainController instructs the MainModel to load the data file. Doing so, it validates the file's content against the corresponding XML schema. A similar procedure is followed to load the card data. Once both files are loaded and validated, the Proceed button is enabled.

When the user selects it, the MainModel creates a new thread to populate the (U)SIM. While this thread is running, the Proceed button is again disabled and the actions the user can take on the interface are limited.

5.1 Thread Processing

When the thread is created, it first parses the validated XML card information and stores it in the registry. It then parses and processes the validated XML data entries, writing them to the (U)SIM. During the data parsing process, the thread requests different information from the registry, like the PIN codes or other characteristics of (U)SIM being populated. Figure 13 illustrates the process.

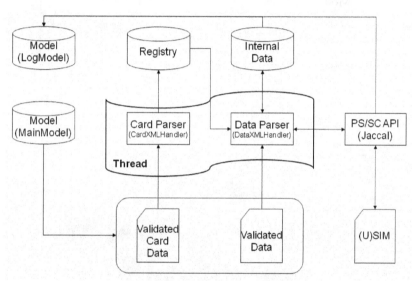

Figure 13: Thread Processing

When the data parser encounters a new entry, it creates a new object to contain the data. For example, if an entry <ef_imsi> is read, the parser creates a java object IMSI (i.e., "IMSI.java") and populates it with the data from the entry. When the end of the entry, "</ef_imsi>," is encountered, the parser requests the IMSI object for an APDU-formatted version of the IMSI to send to the (U)SIM via the Jaccal API. It also requests a human-readable version of the IMSI to record into the log model, which in turn stores it for potential rendering in the user interface.

5.2 Logging

The logging system consists of storage space for events, plus a filter determining which of these events, depending on their severity, are made available to other components of the application. Elements running in different threads may want to log events simultaneously. Therefore, the methods of the LogModel are synchronized (i.e., thread-safe).

The filter is initialized at start up and the different levels of severity are registered. A label is assigned to each severity level, for eventual display in the user interface. The smaller the number is, the higher the level of severity.

Internal namespace identifiers are then registered. They are used to build a map between internally used, severity level identifiers and attributes of the severity level (i.e., mainly for a code to indicate text color). Components of the application can start logging events once registration is done, using the internal severity level identifiers to describe the severity of the event. Figure 14 summarizes the coding steps involved.

```
LogModel logModel = new LogModel();

logModel.registerSeverity( "Severity Label", 1 );

logModel.registerNamespace( "err", "#FF0000", 1 );

logModel.log( "err", "Error message", true );
```

Figure 14: Coding Example

6. Code Modifications

SIMfill can be modified by users to fit their specific needs. The java classfiles are included in the distribution. They can also be studied to gain further insight into SIMfill's operation. The key components of SIMfill are listed in Figure 15. Note that modifications made to the code may also require changes to the schema definitions and reference test data.

Table 2: Key SIMfill Components

Identifier	Component
com.simfill.gui	The classes for the model, controller, and view components comprising the user interface
com.simfill	The classes for the registry and the parser thread
com.simfill.SimFill	The entry point of the application
com.simfill.PCSC	The PC/SC abstraction layer
com.simfill.gsm	The classes for internal data objects

One foreseeable change is to have SIMfill support an EF directly as a named EF, such as those shown in Table 1, in lieu of using the generic EF, RAW, which is identified and populated through its 16-bit file identifier. To make such a change, several steps are required. The first step is to define the schema description for the new XML data entry, using the W3C conventions. Updating the XML schema file, data.xsd, with that definition allows an XML file containing the new data to be created and validated, and sets the foundation for the remaining steps.

The second step is to add new states to the parsing automaton embodied in the DataXMLHandler class. These states are required to provide the means to parse the new data entries and translate them into internal data objects. Parsing is performed using a Simple API for XML (SAX) parser, which is event based. When XML features are encountered, such as the start and end tags of XML elements, an event is triggered, which can be reported via an interface routine. For instance, SIMfill implements the startElement() and endElement() interface routines to keep track of the state of the parsing via a pushdown stack. The startElement() routine pushes a token on the stack for opening tags, and the endElement() pops off a token and matches it with closing tags. Depending on the element, other operations, such as change of directory, data object creation, or writing to the identity module, can also be performed before returning control to the SAX parser. Similarly, SIMfill also implements the characters() routine to read and process data encountered by the SAX parser. Perhaps the easiest way to prepare new states for parsing is to review the cases already coded and use them as a starting point.

The final step is to prepare a new internal data object for the EF in question. If the file is transparent, then the object must inherit the TransparentFile class. Otherwise, the file is linear fixed or cyclic and must inherit the LinearFixedFile class, which is applicable to both of them. Methods inherited from these classes, toHex and toString, must then be implemented in SIMfill. These two methods are used respectively to return the data in the GSM APDU format and to return the data in a human-readable format suitable for logging.

Another possible area for change may be to support other types of developer identity modules. As mentioned earlier, developer identity modules provide the means to populate a broader range of EFs, once Administrative access is gained through authentication. Note that by default Jaccal supports only CHV reference identifiers (CHVRefIds) for PIN1 and PIN2 verification. An extended class was created for SIMfill to convey additional parameters containing ADM authentication values 1 to 4 (see GSMVerifiyCHVEx.java). This change was used for the Gemplus GemXplore (U)SIM and should also work for other developer identity modules that use this non-proprietary method for ADM authentication.

Developer identity modules may use a proprietary method for authentication, which in turn will require a more substantial extension to Jaccal to convey the proprietary APDU content. For example, to support the Axalto SIMagination (U)SIM, a proprietary ADPU was implemented for SIMfill (see AxaltoVerifyKey.java). Information needed to implement ADM authentication is typically available from the (U)SIM manufacturer. As suggested previously, the existing code can also be followed as a model for adding support for other types of identity modules.

7.   References

[3GPP07]   Specification of the Subscriber Identity Module - Mobile Equipment (SIM - ME) interface, 3rd Generation Partnership Project, TS 11.11 V8.14.0 (Release 1999), Technical Specification, June 2007, <URL: http://www.3gpp.org/ftp/Specs/archive/11_series/11.11/1111-8e0.zip>.

[3GPP09a]   Technical Specification Group Core Network and Terminals - Technical realization of the Short Message Service (SMS), 3rd Generation Partnership Project, TS 23.040 V9.0.0 (Release 9), Technical Specification, June 2009, <URL: http://www.3gpp.org/ftp/Specs/archive/23_series/23.040/23040-900.zip>.

[3GPP09b]   Technical Specification Group Core Network and Terminals - Numbering, addressing and identification, 3rd Generation Partnership Project, TS 23.003 V8.5.0 (Release 8), Technical Specification, June 2009, <URL: http://www.3gpp.org/ftp/Specs/archive/23_series/23.003/23003-850.zip>.

[3GPP09c]   Technical Specification Group Core Network and Terminals - SIM/USIM internal and external interworking aspects, 3rd Generation Partnership Project, TR 31.900 V8.0.0 (Release 8), Technical Specification, February 2009, <URL: http://www.3gpp.org/ftp/Specs/archive/31_series/31.900/31900-800.zip>.

[3GPP09d]Technical Specification Group Core Network and Terminals - Alphabets and language-specific information, 3rd Generation Partnership Project, TS 23.038 V9.0.0 (Release 9), Technical Specification, September 2009, <URL: http://www.3gpp.org/ftp/Specs/archive/23_series/23.038/23038-900.zip >.

[IS10646]   Information technology — Universal Multiple-Octet Coded Character Set (UCS), International Standard (IS), ISO/IEC 10646, December 15, 2003, <URL: http://standards.iso.org/ittf/PubliclyAvailableStandards/index.html>.

[ISO639]   Codes for the Representation of Names of Languages-Part 2, ISO 639-2, November 7, 2008, <URL: http://www.loc.gov/standards/iso639-2/php/code_list.php>.

[Jan06]   Wayne Jansen, Rick Ayers, Forensic Software Tools for Cell Phone Subscriber Identity Modules, Conference on Digital Forensics, Association of Digital Forensics, Security, and Law (ADFSL), April 2006, <URL: http://csrc.nist.gov/groups/SNS/mobile_security/documents/mobile_forensics/JDFSL-proceedings2006-fin.pdf>.

[Jan09]   Wayne Jansen, Aurélien Delaitre, Mobile Forensic Reference Materials: A Methodology and Reification, NIST IR 7617, October 2009, <URL: http://csrc.nist.gov/publications/nistir/ir7617/nistir-7617.pdf>

Appendix A: XML Data Representation Examples

This appendix explains, through a series of examples, the XML representation used by SIMfill for specifying the contents of elementary files to be populated. It also provides a brief overview of the organization of SIM file system. As an aid to the reader, specific references to the relevant section of the prevailing GSM SIM standard (i.e., [3GPP07]) are given in braces throughout this appendix (e.g., {10.1.1}).

A.1.0 File Hierarchy

The file system for Subscriber Identity Modules consists of the following elements defined in the GSM specifications:

- The root directory or Master File (MF)

- Directories under the MF called Dedicated Files (DF)

- Elementary Files (EF)

SIMfill can populate the following EFs, which are listed below under their respective directories to reflect the hierarchy defined in the standard [3GPP07]:

MF (Master file {10.1})

       EF_ICCID (ICC Identification {10.1.1})
       EF_ELP (Extended Language Preference {10.1.2})

       DF_GSM (for both DF_GSM and DF_DCS1800 {10.3})
             EF_LP (Language Preference {10.3.1})
             EF_IMSI (International Mobile Subscriber Identity {10.3.2})
             EF_PLMNsel (PLMN selector {10.3.4})
             EF_SST (SIM Service Table {10.3.7})
             EF_SPN (Service Provider Name {10.3.11})
             EF_FPLMN (Forbidden PLMNs {10.3.16})
             EF_LOCI (Location Information {10.3.17})
             EF_AD (Administrative Data {10.3.18})
             EF_PHASE (Phase identification {10.3.19})
             EF_LOCIGPRS (GPRS Location Information {10.3.33})

       DF_TELECOM ({10.5})
             EF_ADN (Abbreviated Dialing Numbers {10.5.1})
             EF_FDN (Fixed Dialing Numbers {10.5.2})
             EF_SMS (Short Message Service {10.5.3})
             EF_MSISDN (MSISDN {10.5.5})
             EF_LND (Last Number Dialed {10.5.8})
             EF_SDN (Service Dialing Numbers {10.5.9})

EF_EXT1 (Extension 1 {10.5.10})
EF_EXT2 (Extension 2 {10.5.11})
EF_EXT3 (Extension 3 {10.5.12})
EF_EXT4 (Extension 4 {10.5.14})

SIMfill can also populate any EF defined in the GSM specifications, including the ones listed above, using the following generic pseudo EF:

EF_RAW (See section A.5.0)

The XML content representation required by SIMfill to populate these EFs is discussed in the sections that follow.

A.2.0 Master File

The MF forms the root of the XML document, just as it represents the root of the SIM's file system {10.1}. The MF takes the following optional subnodes in any order:

- "ef_iccid": Describes the ICCID of the SIM.
- "ef_elp": Describes the extended language preferences.
- "df_gsm": Subdirectory containing network information (used for both DF_GSM and DF_DCS1800).
- "df_telecom": Subdirectory containing service information.

Basic example of structure:

```
<?xml version='1.0' encoding='UTF-8'?>
<mf>
        <ef_elp></ef_elp>
        <df_gsm>
        </df_gsm>
</mf>
```

A.2.1 EF_ICCID

EF_ICCID {10.1.1} is used to specify the identification number of the SIM. It takes a decimal number between 0 and 20 digits long. For example:

```
<?xml version='1.0' encoding='UTF-8'?>
<mf>
        <ef_iccid>00112233445566778899</ef_iccid>
</mf>
```

A.2.2 EF_ELP

EF_ELP {10.1.2} is used to specify the preferred languages of the user in order of priority. It takes two different subnodes, which can be mixed and repeated arbitrarily:

- "elp": A 2-letter language code encoded in the GSM 7-bit alphabet [3GPP09d].
- "empty": Used to insert an empty record in the file.

In this example, the preferred languages are English, followed by an empty slot, and then French:

```
<?xml version='1.0' encoding='UTF-8'?>
<mf>
        <ef_elp>
                <elp>en</elp>
                <empty/>
                <elp>fr</elp>
        </ef_elp>
</mf>
```

The list of language codes is described in ISO 639-2 [ISO639].

A.3.0   DF_GSM and DF_DCS1800

DF_GSM {10.3} contains network related information. Note that specifying data in DF_GSM writes only to DF_GSM on the SIM. Nonetheless, the SIM is expected to mirror DF_GSM and DF_DCS1800, making the latter identical to the former.

This node takes the following subnodes, in any order:

- "ef_lp": Language Preference of the user.
- "ef_imsi": International Mobile Subscriber Identity.
- "ef_plmnsel": PLMN selector.
- "ef_sst": SIM Service Table.
- "ef_spn": Service Provider Name.
- "ef_fplmn": Forbidden PLMNs.
- "ef_loci": Location Information.
- "ef_ad": Administrative Data.
- "ef_phase": Phase identification.
- "ef_locigprs": GPRS Location data.

Basic example of structure:

```
<?xml version='1.0' encoding='UTF-8'?>
<mf>
        <df_gsm>
                <ef_imsi></ef_imsi>
                <ef_plmnsel></ef_plmnsel>
        </df_gsm>
</mf>
```

24

A.3.1 EF_LP

EF_LP {10.3.1} is used to specify the preferred languages of the user in order of priority. It takes two different subnodes, which can be mixed and repeated arbitrarily:

- "lp": A language name, as listed below.
- "empty": Used to insert an empty record in the file.

In this example, the favorite language is left empty, the second favorite is German, then another empty slot, followed by English and Hebrew:

```
<?xml version='1.0' encoding='UTF-8'?>
<mf>
        <df_gsm>
                <ef_lp>
                        <empty/>
                        <lp>german</lp>
                        <empty/>
                        <lp>english</lp>
                        <lp>hebrew</lp>
                </ef_lp>
        </df_gsm>
</mf>
```

The list of language codes is described in [3GPP09d] 5. The aliases for these codes are:

- "german"
- "english"
- "italian"
- "french"
- "spanish"
- "dutch"
- "swedish"
- "danish"
- "portuguese"
- "finnish"
- "norwegian"
- "greek"
- "turkish"
- "hungarian"
- "polish"
- "unspecified"
- "czech"
- "hebrew"

- "arabic"
- "russian"

A.3.2 EF_IMSI

EF_IMSI {10.3.2} is used to specify the International Mobile Subscriber Identity. It takes a decimal number between 0 and 15 digits long. For example:

```
<?xml version='1.0' encoding='UTF-8'?>
<mf>
        <df_gsm>
                <ef_imsi>887766554433221</ef_imsi>
        </df_gsm>
</mf>
```

A.3.3 EF_PLMNsel

EF_PLMNsel {10.3.4} is used to specify the preferred networks of the user in order of priority. It takes two subnodes, which can be mixed and repeated arbitrarily:

- "plmn": Public Land Mobile Network, described below.
- "empty": Used to insert an empty record in the file.

In this example, one PLMN is specified, followed by an empty slot, and then another PLMN:

```
<?xml version='1.0' encoding='UTF-8'?>
<mf>
        <df_gsm>
                <ef_plmnsel>
                        <plmn></plmn>
                        <empty/>
                        <plmn></plmn>
                </ef_plmnsel>
        </df_gsm>
</mf>
```

Each PLMN subnode describes one network. It has two subnodes:

- "mcc": Mobile Country Code, a 3-digit decimal number.
- "mnc": Mobile Network Code, a 2- or 3-digit decimal number.

Below is a more complete example. The first PLMN belongs to T-Mobile USA, followed by an empty slot, and by a PLMN belonging to Orange France:

```
<?xml version='1.0' encoding='UTF-8'?>
<mf>
        <df_gsm>
                <ef_plmnsel>
```

```
                    <plmn>
                            <mcc>310</mcc>
                            <mnc>26</mnc>
                    </plmn>
                    <empty/>
                    <plmn>
                            <mcc>208</mcc>
                            <mnc>01</mnc>
                    </plmn>
                </ef_plmnsel>
            </df_gsm>
    </mf>
```

A.3.4 EF_SST

EF_SST {10.3.7} is used to set up the SIM Service Table. It takes a sequence of the subnode "service", which can be repeated arbitrarily:

```
<?xml version='1.0' encoding='UTF-8'?>
<mf>
        <df_gsm>
                <ef_sst>
                        <service></service>
                        <service></service>
                        <service></service>
                </ef_sst>
        </df_gsm>
</mf>
```

Each "service" subnode describes one service. It takes three subnodes:

- "number": Number of the service. A table associating the service to its number is provided in the standard {10.3.7}.
- "allocated": Describes whether a service is allocated or not.
- "activated": Describes whether an allocated service is activated or not.

In the following example, service number 1 (CHV disable function) is allocated, but not activated. Service number 2 (Abbreviated Dialing Numbers) is allocated an activated. All other services are automatically set to unallocated and deactivated.

```
<?xml version='1.0' encoding='UTF-8'?>
<mf>
        <df_gsm>
                <ef_sst>
                        <service>
                                <number>1</number>
                                <allocated>true</allocated>
                                <activated>false</activated>
                        </service>
                        <service>
                                <number>2</number>
                                <allocated>true</allocated>
```

27

```
                              <activated>true</activated>
                    </service>
               </ef_sst>
          </df_gsm>
     </mf>
```

Note: A service must be allocated to be activated. By default, a service which is not explicitly specified is set to unallocated and deactivated.

A.3.5 EF_SPN

EF_SPN {10.3.11} is used to specify the Service Provider Name. It takes two subnodes:

- "display": Display condition. It can be either "required" or "not required".
- "spn": Service Provider Name. It is a string that can be encoded either in the default GSM 7-bit alphabet or in UCS2. To specify which encoding to use, one can set the XML attribute "enc" to "default" for 7-bit encoding or "ucs2" for UCS2 encoding. If no encoding is explicitly specified, the 7-bit encoding is used by default.

In this example, the display of the SPN is required. The SPN is set to "NIST" and encoded in UCS2:

```
<?xml version='1.0' encoding='UTF-8'?>
<mf>
     <df_gsm>
          <ef_spn>
               <display>required</display>
               <spn enc="ucs2">NIST</spn>
          </ef_spn>
     </df_gsm>
</mf>
```

In this example, the display of the SPN is not required. The SPN is set to "NIST" and encoded in the default 7-bit alphabet:

```
<?xml version='1.0' encoding='UTF-8'?>
<mf>
     <df_gsm>
          <ef_spn>
               <display>not required</display>
               <spn>NIST</spn>
          </ef_spn>
     </df_gsm>
</mf>
```

A.3.6 EF_FPLMN

EF_FPLMN {10.3.16} is used to specify the forbidden PLMNs the mobile equipment (i.e., the phone handset) should not try to access. It has the same structure as EF_PLMNsel (see section A.3.3).

28

In this example, the first forbidden PLMN belongs to T-Mobile USA, followed by an empty slot, and by a forbidden PLMN belonging to Orange France:

```xml
<?xml version='1.0' encoding='UTF-8'?>
<mf>
      <df_gsm>
            <ef_fplmn>
                  <plmn>
                        <mcc>310</mcc>
                        <mnc>26</mnc>
                  </plmn>
                  <empty/>
                  <plmn>
                        <mcc>208</mcc>
                        <mnc>01</mnc>
                  </plmn>
            </ef_fplmn>
      </df_gsm>
</mf>
```

A.3.7 EF_LOCI

EF_LOCI {10.3.17} is used to specify the location information. It takes four subnodes:

- "tmsi": The Temporary Mobile Subscriber Identity is an 8-digit hexadecimal number.
- "lai": The Location Area Information is described below.
- "time": TMSI time is a 2-digit hexadecimal number.
- "status": Location update status, as described below.

The subnode "lai" takes three subnodes:

- "mcc": Mobile Country Code, a 3-digit decimal number.
- "mnc": Mobile Network Code, a 2- or 3-digit decimal number.
- "lac": Location Area Code, a 4-digit hexadecimal number.

The subnode "status" can take the following values:
- "updated"
- "not updated"
- "plmn not allowed"
- "location area not allowed"
- "reserved"

Below is an example representation:

29

```
<?xml version='1.0' encoding='UTF-8'?>
<mf>
      <df_gsm>
            <ef_loci>
                  <tmsi>a1b2c3d4</tmsi>
                  <lai>
                        <mcc>310</mcc>
                        <mnc>26</mnc>
                        <lac>a1b2</lac>
                  </lai>
                  <time>00</time>
                  <status>updated</status>
            </ef_loci>
      </df_gsm>
</mf>
```

A.3.8 EF_AD

EF_AD {10.3.18} is used to specify miscellaneous administrative information. It takes three subnodes:

- "opmode": The operation mode, which is described below.
- "ofm": The Operational Feature Monitor (OFM), described below.
- "mnclen": The length of the MNC in the IMSI. It takes a number, either "2" or "3". If another value needs to be used, it can be done within the "ef_raw" section of "ef_gsm".

The subnode "opmode" describes the mode in which the mobile station (MS) is working. It can take one of the following values:

- "normal"
- "type approval"
- "normal specific"
- "type approval specific"
- "maintenance"
- "celltest"

The subnode "ofm" can be either "activated" or "disabled". Refer to {10.3.18} for more information.

In the following example, the MS works in normal mode, with OFM disabled and the MNC in the IMSI is 3 digits long:

```
<?xml version='1.0' encoding='UTF-8'?>
<mf>
      <df_gsm>
            <ef_ad>
                  <opmode>normal</opmode>
```

30

```
            <ofm>disabled</ofm>
            <mnclen>3</mnclen>
        </ef_ad>
    </df_gsm>
</mf>
```

A.3.9 EF_PHASE

EF_PHASE {10.3.19} is used to specify the phase of the SIM. It takes a 2-digit hexadecimal value.

In this example, the SIM's phase is set to 2+:

```
<?xml version='1.0' encoding='UTF-8'?>
<mf>
    <df_gsm>
        <ef_phase>03</ef_phase>
    </df_gsm>
</mf>
```

A.3.10 EF_LOCIGPRS

EF_LOCIGPRS {10.3.33} is used to specify the location information related to GPRS. It takes four subnodes:

- "ptmsi": The Packet Temporary Mobile Subscriber Identity (P-TMSI) is an 8-digit hexadecimal number.
- "signature": The P-TMSI signature. It takes a 6-digit hexadecimal value.
- "rai": The Routing Area Information is described below.
- "status": Location update status, as described below.

The subnode "rai" takes four subnodes:

- "mcc": Mobile Country Code, a 3-digit decimal number.
- "mnc": Mobile Network Code, a 2- or 3-digit decimal number.
- "lac": Location Area Code, a 4-digit hexadecimal number.
- "rac": Routing Area Code, a 2-digit hexadecimal number.

The subnode "status" can take the following values:

- "updated"
- "not updated"
- "plmn not allowed"
- "location area not allowed"
- "reserved"

31

Below is an example representation:

```xml
<?xml version='1.0' encoding='UTF-8'?>
<mf>
        <df_gsm>
                <ef_locigprs>
                        <ptmsi>a1b2c3d4</ptmsi>
                        <signature>ffffff</signature>
                        <rai>
                                <mcc>310</mcc>
                                <mnc>26</mnc>
                                <lac>a1b2</lac>
                                <rac>a1</rac>
                        </rai>
                        <status>updated</status>
                </ef_locigprs>
        </df_gsm>
</mf>
```

A.4.0 DF_TELECOM

DF_TELECOM {10.5} contains service related information. It takes the following subnodes, in any order:

- "ef_adn": Abbreviated Dialing Numbers.
- "ef_fdn": Fixed Dialing Numbers.
- "ef_sms: Short Messages.
- "ef_msisdn": MS International ISDN Number.
- "ef_lnd": Last Number Dialed.
- "ef_sdn": Service Dialing Numbers.
- "ef_ext1": Extension 1.
- "ef_ext2": Extension 2.
- "ef_ext3": Extension 3.
- "ef_ext4": Extension 4.

Below is a basic example of the structure:

```xml
<?xml version='1.0' encoding='UTF-8'?>
<mf>
        <df_telecom>
                <ef_raw></ef_raw>
                <ef_adn></ef_adn>
        </df_telecom>
</mf>
```

A.4.1 EF_ADN

EF_ADN {10.5.1} is used to specify the abbreviated dialing number (i.e., the phone book). It takes two different subnodes, which can be mixed and repeated arbitrarily:

- "contact": A contact contains a set of information, as described below.
- "empty": Used to insert an empty record in the file.

The subnode "contact" has three or four subnodes:

- "description": The name of the contact. It is a string that can be encoded either in the default GSM 7-bit alphabet or in UCS2. To specify which encoding to use, one can set the XML attribute "enc" to "default" for 7-bit encoding or "ucs2" for UCS2 encoding. If no encoding is explicitly specified, the 7-bit encoding is used by default.
- "address": Contains the phone number information of the contact, as described below.
- "capability": Index pointing to a record of EF_CCP. It take a decimal number between 0 and 255. This subnode is optional.
- "extension": The index of additional data that are stored in EF_EXT1 (see the example below). It takes a decimal number between 0 and 255. This subnode is optional.

The subnode "address" takes three subnodes:

- "ton": The Type of Number. The possible values are listed below.
- "npi": Numbering Plan Identifier. The possible values are listed below.
- "number": The phone number of the contact. It takes a 0- to 20-digit decimal number.

The subnode "ton" can take one of the following values:

- "unknown"
- "international"
- "national"
- "network specific"
- "subscriber"
- "alphanumeric"
- "abbreviated"
- "reserved"

The subnode "npi" can take one of the following values:

- "unknown"
- "telephone"
- "data"
- "telex"
- "service center specific 1"
- "service center specific 2"
- "national"
- "private"
- "ermes"
- "reserved"

Detailed information about these values is available in the standard {10.5.1}.

In the following example, the phone book contains three entries. The first is labeled "Contact 1" (encoded using the default 7-bit alphabet) and its phone number is "3019758000" (national). The second entry is an empty slot. The third is labeled "Contact 2" (encoded in UCS2) and its phone number is "13019758000" (international), with extra data in the second record of EF_EXT1 (to be specified separately).

```xml
<?xml version='1.0' encoding='UTF-8'?>
<mf>
        <df_telecom>
                <ef_adn>
                        <contact>
                                <description>Contact 1</description>
                                <address>
                                        <ton>national</ton>
                                        <npi>telephone</npi>
                                        <number>3019758000</number>
                                </address>
                        </contact>
                        <empty/>
                        <contact>
                                <description enc="ucs2">Contact
2</description>
                                <address>
                                        <ton>international</ton>
                                        <npi>telephone</npi>
                                        <number>13019758000</number>
                                </address>
                                <extension>2</extension>
                        </contact>
                </ef_adn>
        </df_telecom>
</mf>
```

A.4.2 EF_FDN

EF_FDN {10.5.2} is used to specify the fixed dialed numbers. It has the same structure as EF_ADN (see section A.4.1).

In the following example, the phone book contains three entries. The first is labeled "Fixed number 1" (encoded using the default 7-bit alphabet) and its phone number is "3019758000" (national). The second entry is an empty slot. The third is labeled "Fixed number 2" (encoded in UCS2) and its phone number is "13019758000" (international), with extra data in the second record of EF_EXT2 (to be specified separately).

```xml
<?xml version='1.0' encoding='UTF-8'?>
<mf>
        <df_telecom>
                <ef_fdn>
                        <contact>
                                <description>Fixed number 1</description>
                                <address>
                                        <ton>national</ton>
                                        <npi>telephone</npi>
                                        <number>3019758000</number>
                                </address>
                        </contact>
                        <empty/>
                        <contact>
                                <description enc="ucs2">Fixed number
2</description>
                                <address>
                                        <ton>international</ton>
                                        <npi>telephone</npi>
                                        <number>13019758000</number>
                                </address>
                                <extension>2</extension>
                        </contact>
                </ef_fdn>
        </df_telecom>
</mf>
```

A.4.3 EF_SMS

EF_SMS {10.5.3} is used to specify short messages. It takes three different subnodes, which can be mixed and repeated arbitrarily:

- "deliver": For incoming messages, as described below.
- "submit": For outgoing messages, as described below.
- "empty": Used to insert an empty record in the file.

Example structure:

```xml
<?xml version='1.0' encoding='UTF-8'?>
<mf>
```

35

```
<df_telecom>
     <ef_sms>
          <deliver></deliver>
          <empty/>
          <submit></submit>
          <deliver></deliver>
     </ef_sms>
</df_telecom>
</mf>
```

The subnode "deliver" takes the following subnodes:

- "status": Status of the message, as described below.

- "sca": Service Center Address. It takes one subnode of type "address", as described in EF_ADN (see section A.4.1).

- "mms": Flag indicating if there are More Messages to Send. It takes either "true" or "false".

- "sri": The Status Report Indicator indicates whether a report is requested or not. It takes either "true" or "false".

- "rp": This flag indicates if a Reply Path is specified. It takes either "true" or "false".

- "oa": Originated Address or address of the sender. It takes one subnode of type "address", as described in EF_ADN (see section A.4.1).

- "dcs": The Data Encoding Scheme is used to specify which encoding is used for the text data. It can be either "default" for the 7-bit alphabet or "ucs2" for UCS2 encoding.

- "scts": The Service Center Time Stamp is a date set by the service center. Its format is "YYYY-MM-DD hh:mm:ss +OOoo", where "YYYY" is the year, "MM" the month of the year, "DD" the day of the month, "hh" the hour of the day, "mm" the minute of the hour, "ss" the second of the minute, and "+OOoo" the time difference compared to GMT, "OO" being the number of hours and "oo" the number of minutes. If the time difference is negative, the "+" should be replaced by a "-".

- "udh": User Data Header, as described below. This node is optional.

- "ud": User Data, a string containing the message. Its maximum length depends on the encoding used (see "dcs" above), on the user data header included and on the size of other parameters in the header.

In the example below, an incoming message is specified. It has not been read. The service center's number is "+19703769313". No more messages are waiting to be delivered, no report is requested, no reply path has been specified. The sender's phone number is "3019750000". The message is encoded using the default 7-bit alphabet. The service center's time stamp is June 24, 2005 at 00:13:24 GMT-4. And the text message is "This is an incoming message."

```xml
<?xml version='1.0' encoding='UTF-8'?>
<mf>
    <df_telecom>
        <ef_sms>
            <deliver>
                <status>not read</status>
                <sca>
                    <address>
                        <ton>international</ton>
                        <npi>telephone</npi>
                        <number>19703769313</number>
                    </address>
                </sca>
                <mms>false</mms>
                <sri>false</sri>
                <rp>false</rp>
                <oa>
                    <address>
                        <ton>national</ton>
                        <npi>telephone</npi>
                        <number>3019750000</number>
                    </address>
                </oa>
                <dcs>default</dcs>
                <scts>2005-06-24 00:13:24 -0400</scts>
                <ud>This is an incoming message.</ud>
            </deliver>
        </ef_sms>
    </df_telecom>
</mf>
```

The subnode "submit" takes the following subnodes:

- "status": Status of the message, as described below.

- "sca": Service Center Address. It takes one subnode of type "address", as described in EF_ADN (see section A.4.1).

- "rd": This flag indicates whether or not duplicate messages should be rejected. It takes either "true" or "false".

- "srr": Indicates if a Status Report is Requested. It takes either "true" of "false".

- "rp": This flag indicates if a Reply Path is specified. It takes either "true" or "false".

- "mr": Message reference. It takes a decimal number between 0 and 255.

- "da": Destination Address or address of the receiver. It takes one subnode of type "address", as described in EF_ADN (see section A.4.1).

- "dcs": The Data Encoding Scheme is used to specify which encoding is used for the text data. It can be either "default" for the 7-bit alphabet or "ucs2" for UCS2 encoding.

- "udh": User Data Header, as described below. This node is optional.

- "ud": User Data, a string containing the message. Its maximum length depends on the encoding used (see "dcs" above), on the user data header included, and on the size of other parameters in the header.

In the example below, an outgoing message is specified. It has been sent. The service center's number is "+19703769313". The service center is asked to reject duplicates, no status report is requested, and no reply path has been specified. The message reference is 122. The receiver's phone number is "+33123456789". The message is encoded in UCS2. And the text message is "This is an outgoing message."

```xml
<?xml version='1.0' encoding='UTF-8'?>
<mf>
    <df_telecom>
        <ef_sms>
            <submit>
                <status>sent</status>
                <sca>
                    <address>
                        <ton>international</ton>
                        <npi>telephone</npi>
                        <number>19703769313</number>
                    </address>
                </sca>
                <rd>true</rd>
                <srr>false</srr>
                <rp>false</rp>
                <mr>122</mr>
                <da>
                    <address>
                        <ton>international</ton>
                        <npi>data</npi>
                        <number>33123456789</number>
                    </address>
                </da>
                <dcs>ucs2</dcs>
                <ud>This is an outgoing message.</ud>
            </submit>
        </ef_sms>
    </df_telecom>
</mf>
```

The subnode "status" describes de status of the message. It can take one of the following values:

- "free" or "deleted": The message will be stored in the record, but will be marked as deleted.
- "read": The message has been read.
- " not read": The message has not been read.
- "sent": The message has been sent.
- "not sent": The message has not been sent.

Note that both types of message ("submit" and "deliver") can take any of these values, even though it would not make much sense to have an unread outgoing message or a sent incoming message.

The subnode "udh", listing the user data headers, can take the following subnodes, which can be repeated and mixed arbitrarily:

- "concat": This header indicates that the message is split into several segments.
- "smlimg": This header is used to insert an small image (16x16) in the message.
- "lrgimg": This header is used to insert an large image (32x32) in the message.

The subnode "concat" has three attributes:

- "ref": The reference of the message. It takes a decimal number between 0 and 255.
- "max": Is the total number of segments in the concatenated message. It takes a decimal number between 0 and 255.
- "seq": Is the sequence number of the current segment. It takes a decimal number between 0 and 255.

Example of a concatenated message divided in two segments is given below (note that they can be stored in any order in EF_SMS):

```xml
<?xml version='1.0' encoding='UTF-8'?>
<mf>
    <df_telecom>
        <ef_sms>
            <submit>
                <status>sent</status>
                <sca>
                    <address>
                        <ton>international</ton>
                        <npi>telephone</npi>
                        <number>19703769313</number>
                    </address>
                </sca>
                <rd>true</rd>
                <srr>false</srr>
                <rp>false</rp>
                <mr>122</mr>
                <da>
                    <address>
                        <ton>international</ton>
                        <npi>data</npi>
                        <number>33123456789</number>
                    </address>
                </da>
```

39

```
                        <dcs>default</dcs>
                        <udh>
                                <concat ref='21' max='2' seq='1'/>
                        </udh>
                        <ud>Concatenated message 21 part 1/2</ud>
                </submit>
                <submit>
                        <status>sent</status>
                        <sca>
                                <address>
                                        <ton>international</ton>
                                        <npi>telephone</npi>
                                        <number>19703769313</number>
                                </address>
                        </sca>
                        <rd>true</rd>
                        <srr>false</srr>
                        <rp>false</rp>
                        <mr>123</mr>
                        <da>
                                <address>
                                        <ton>international</ton>
                                        <npi>data</npi>
                                        <number>33123456789</number>
                                </address>
                        </da>
                        <dcs>default</dcs>
                        <udh>
                                <concat ref='21' max='2' seq='2'/>
                        </udh>
                        <ud>Concatenated message 21 part 2/2</ud>
                </submit>
            </ef_sms>
        </df_telecom>
    </mf>
```

The subnodes "smlimg" and "lrgimg" takes the following attributes:

- "pos": The position at which the image should be inserted in the text. It takes a positive integer.
- "file": Path to the image to be included in the text message.

The example below shows an incoming message in which a large image is inserted:

```
    <?xml version='1.0' encoding='UTF-8'?>
    <mf>
        <df_telecom>
            <ef_sms>
                <deliver>
                        <status>not read</status>
                        <sca>
                                <address>
                                        <ton>international</ton>
                                        <npi>telephone</npi>
```

```
                                        <number>19703769313</number>
                                </address>
                        </sca>
                        <mms>false</mms>
                        <sri>false</sri>
                        <rp>false</rp>
                        <oa>
                                <address>
                                        <ton>national</ton>
                                        <npi>telephone</npi>
                                        <number>3019750000</number>
                                </address>
                        </oa>
                        <dcs>default</dcs>
                        <scts>2005-06-24 00:13:24 -0400</scts>
                        <udh>
                                <lrgimg pos='1'
file='./data/lrgimg.bmp'/>
                        </udh>
                        <ud>()</ud>
                </deliver>
        </ef_sms>
    </df_telecom>
</mf>
```

A.4.4 EF_MSISDN

EF_MSISDN {10.5.5} is used to specify MSISDNs related to the subscriber. It has the same structure as EF_ADN (see section A.4.1).

In the following example, the phone book contains three entries. The first is labeled "MSISDN 1" (encoded using the default 7-bit alphabet) and its phone number is "3019758000" (national). The second entry is an empty slot. The third is labeled "MSISDN 2" (encoded in UCS2) and its phone number is "13019758000" (international), with extra data in the second record of EF_EXT1 (to be specified separately).

```
<?xml version='1.0' encoding='UTF-8'?>
<mf>
    <df_telecom>
        <ef_msisdn>
            <contact>
                <description>MSISDN 1</description>
                <address>
                    <ton>national</ton>
                    <npi>telephone</npi>
                    <number>3019758000</number>
                </address>
            </contact>
            <empty/>
            <contact>
                <description enc="ucs2">MSISDN
2</description>
                <address>
                    <ton>international</ton>
```

```
                              <npi>telephone</npi>
                              <number>13019758000</number>
                      </address>
                      <extension>2</extension>
                </contact>
            </ef_msisdn>
        </df_telecom>
    </mf>
```

A.4.5 EF_LND

EF_LND {10.5.8} is used to specify the list of last dialed numbers. It has the same structure as EF_ADN (see section A.4.1), except it does not accept the "empty" subnode. This is due to the fact the EF_LND is a cyclic file, unlike EF_ADN, which is a linear file.

In the following example, the call log contains two entries. The first is labeled "2nd call" (encoded using the default 7-bit alphabet) and its phone number is "3019758000" (national). The second is labeled "1st call" (encoded in UCS2) and its phone number is "13019758000" (international), with extra data in the second record of EF_EXT1 (to be specified separately).

```
        <?xml version='1.0' encoding='UTF-8'?>
        <mf>
            <df_telecom>
                <ef_lnd>
                    <contact>
                        <description>2nd call</description>
                        <address>
                            <ton>national</ton>
                            <npi>telephone</npi>
                            <number>3019758000</number>
                        </address>
                    </contact>
                    <contact>
                        <description enc="ucs2">1st
call</description>
                        <address>
                            <ton>international</ton>
                            <npi>telephone</npi>
                            <number>13019758000</number>
                        </address>
                        <extension>2</extension>
                    </contact>
                </ef_lnd>
            </df_telecom>
        </mf>
```

A.4.6 EF_SDN

EF_SDN {10.5.9} is used to specify the special service numbers. It has the same structure as EF_ADN (see section A.4.1).

In the following example, the phone book contains three entries. The first is labeled "Special number 1" (encoded using the default 7-bit alphabet) and its phone number is "3019758000" (national). The second entry is an empty slot. The third is labeled "Special number 2" (encoded in UCS2) and its phone number is "13019758000" (international), with extra data in the second record of EF_EXT3 (to be specified separately).

```
<?xml version='1.0' encoding='UTF-8'?>
<mf>
        <df_telecom>
                <ef_sdn>
                        <contact>
                                <description>Special number 1</description>
                                <address>
                                        <ton>national</ton>
                                        <npi>telephone</npi>
                                        <number>3019758000</number>
                                </address>
                        </contact>
                        <empty/>
                        <contact>
                                <description enc="ucs2">Special number
2</description>
                                <address>
                                        <ton>international</ton>
                                        <npi>telephone</npi>
                                        <number>13019758000</number>
                                </address>
                                <extension>2</extension>
                        </contact>
                </ef_sdn>
        </df_telecom>
</mf>
```

A.4.7 EF_EXT1

EF_EXT1 {10.5.10} is used to specify extension data from EF_ADN, EF_MSISDN or EF_LND. It takes two subnodes, which can be mixed and repeated arbitrarily:

■ "additional": Used to specify additional data, as described below.

■ "empty": Used to insert an empty record in the file.

The subnode "additional" takes two subnodes:

■ "data": The extra data, a decimal number up to 20 digits.

■ "extension": An index to another record of EF_EXT1, which means entries can be chained. It takes a decimal number between 0 and 255. This subnode is optional.

43

In this example, the first entry is an empty slot. The second has the extra data "9999". The third contains the extra data "00112233445566778899" and is pointing to the second entry for even more data:

```xml
<?xml version='1.0' encoding='UTF-8'?>
<mf>
        <df_telecom>
                <ef_ext1>
                        <empty/>
                        <additional>
                                <data>9999</data>
                        </additional>
                        <additional>
                                <data>00112233445566778899</data>
                        <extension>2</extension>
                        </additional>
                </ef_ext1>
        </df_telecom>
</mf>
```

A.4.8   EF_EXT2

EF_EXT2 {10.5.11} is used to specify extension data from EF_FDN. It has the same structure as EF_EXT1 (see section A.4.7).

In this example, the first entry is an empty slot. The second holds extra data "9999". The third contains the extra data "00112233445566778899" and is pointing to the second entry for even more data:

```xml
<?xml version='1.0' encoding='UTF-8'?>
<mf>
        <df_telecom>
                <ef_ext2>
                        <empty/>
                        <additional>
                                <data>9999</data>
                        </additional>
                        <additional>
                                <data>00112233445566778899</data>
                                <extension>2</extension>
                        </additional>
                </ef_ext2>
        </df_telecom>
</mf>
```

A.4.9   EF_EXT3

EF_EXT3 {10.5.12} is used to specify extension data from EF_SDN. It has the same structure as EF_EXT1 (see section A.4.7).

44

In this example, the first entry is an empty slot. The second has the extra data "9999". The third contains the extra data "00112233445566778899" and is pointing to the second entry for even more data:

```xml
<?xml version='1.0' encoding='UTF-8'?>
<mf>
        <df_telecom>
                <ef_ext3>
                        <empty/>
                        <additional>
                                <data>9999</data>
                        </additional>
                        <additional>
                                <data>00112233445566778899</data>
                                <extension>2</extension>
                        </additional>
                </ef_ext3>
        </df_telecom>
</mf>
```

A.4.10 EF_EXT4

EF_EXT4 {10.5.14} is used to specify extension data from EF_BDN. It has the same structure as EF_EXT1 (see section A.4.7).

In this example, the first entry is an empty slot. The second has the extra data "9999". The third contains the extra data "00112233445566778899" and is pointing to the second entry for even more data:

```xml
<?xml version='1.0' encoding='UTF-8'?>
<mf>
        <df_telecom>
                <ef_ext4>
                        <empty/>
                        <additional>
                                <data>9999</data>
                        </additional>
                        <additional>
                                <data>00112233445566778899</data>
                                <extension>2</extension>
                        </additional>
                </ef_ext4>
        </df_telecom>
</mf>
```

A.5.0 EF_RAW

EF_RAW is a pseudo file supported in the XML document structure to allow one to populate any file in the directory structure. It is normally reserved for special cases not covered by the other file specifications discussed earlier this document. An EF_RAW entry can be used for EFs at the MF, DF_GSM, and DF_TELECOM levels. Because

EF_RAW is a universal, generic type of subnode, it requires a firm understanding of the SIM file system conventions defined in the GSM standards to apply it correctly.

The following example illustrates the basic structure for employing EF_RAW to populate a file in the DF_GSM directory:

```xml
<?xml version='1.0' encoding='UTF-8'?>
<mf>
        <df_gsm>
                <ef_raw></ef_raw>
        </df_gsm>
</mf>
```

To fully specify EF_RAW for any files in question, additional information is needed. One can populate any type of file supported by the identity module's file system. Three types of files can be specified:

- "transparent" for transparent files {6.4.1}
- "fixed" for linear fixed files {6.4.2}
- "cyclic" for cyclic files {6.4.3}.

These entries can be mixed and repeated arbitrarily to accommodate the structure of any targeted files. For example:

```xml
<?xml version='1.0' encoding='UTF-8'?>
<mf>
        <df_gsm>
                <ef_raw>
                        <transparent></transparent>
                        <fixed></fixed>
                        <transparent></transparent>
                        <cyclic></cyclic>
                </ef_raw>
        </df_gsm>
</mf>
```

A transparent file's entry has two nodes:

- "id": The 16-bit file identifier encoded in hexadecimal.
- "data": The data to store in the file, in hexadecimal. It must match the size of the file on the SIM.

Below is an example instance to populate EF_Kc (Ciphering Key {10.3.3}):

```xml
<?xml version='1.0' encoding='UTF-8'?>
<mf>
        <df_gsm>
                <ef_raw>
                        <transparent>
```

46

```
                        <id>6F20</id>
                        <data>0011223344556677EE</data>
                </transparent>
            </ef_raw>
        </df_gsm>
    </mf>
```

Fixed and cyclic file entries have the same three nodes:

- "id": The 16-bit file identifier encoded in hexadecimal.
- "record": The data to store in the current record, in hexadecimal. It must match the size of a file record on the SIM. Several repetitions of this entry are allowed. The files are populated sequentially, starting at the first record.
- "empty": Used to insert an empty record in the file. It can be repeated.

In this example, EF_SDN (Service Dialing Numbers {10.5.9}) is populated with three entries, one with data, one empty, and another one with data:

```
<?xml version='1.0' encoding='UTF-8'?>
<mf>
        <df_telecom>
            <ef_raw>
                <fixed>
                    <id>6F49</id>

<record>80963F5A465BB691CC97625BF94E8EFFFFFFFFFF0593685703F9FFFFFFF
FFFFFFFFF</record>

                        <empty/>

<record>4E616D65201F7405FFFFFFFFFFFFFFFFFFFFFFFFFFF0BA4212233434414325
476F8FFFF</record>
                </fixed>
            </ef_raw>
        </df_telecom>
    </mf>
```

A.6.0 Encoding Issues

Because a data file is an XML document, certain characters used in the XML syntax need to be represented differently when used for input data, as shown in the table below.

Character	Name	Representation
&	Ampersand	&
<	Lower than	<
>	Greater than	>
"	Quote	"
'	Apostrophe	'

Numeric fields containing data represented using the hexadecimal digits can use either uppercase or lowercase arbitrarily for the letters A through F.

47

SIMfill supports two different encoding schemes for textual data: the default GSM 7-bit alphabet encoding [3GPP09d] and the 16-bit UCS2 encoding [3GPP09d, IS10646]. Only a certain subset of characters can be encoded using the GSM 7-bit alphabet, which is the default encoding. They are mostly Latin characters, plus some special characters, as described in [3GPP09d] 6.2.1. Each of these characters is encoded in a septet (i.e., 7 bits).

Example: This message could be encoded with the 7-bit alphabet.

In addition, extended characters can be used, which are encoded with 2 septets; the first septet being the escape character (0x1b) and the second one the code for the character in an extension table. These extended characters are listed in [3GPP09d] 6.2.1.1., and include such things as the Euro character, left and right braces, and tilde. SIMfill handles extended characters that appear in the XML content and encodes them using two septets.

Example: [This m€ssag€ would r€nquir€ th€ 7~bit €xt€nd€d alphab€t.]

With SIMfill you can also use the back-quote symbol (i.e., `) before a regular character to "escape" into a corresponding location in the extended character table. The standard states that an "escaped" character that is not defined in the extended table should appear as a regular character. For example, while `e would result in the Euro symbol from the extended character set, `f results in f, because no corresponding extended character is defined in the standard.

Example of a mixed string is the following:
      The string: `E`s`c`a`p`e`d` `r`e`g`u`l`a`r` `c`h`a`r`a`c`t`e`r`s
      Should appear as: Escap€d r€gular charact€rs

Note that SIMfill does not support Greek characters in GSM 7-bit alphabet due to charset limitations encountered in its development.

In contrast to the GSM 7-bit encoding, UCS2 can be used to encode almost any possible character, ideogram, or symbol. Each of these characters (i.e., graphemes) is encoded in 16 bits. The complete list of UCS2 characters is described in [IS10646].

A simple example of text using the Japanese katakana and English alphabet is as follows:
ニスツ – NIST

Appendix B: Dataset Content Examples

This appendix illustrates a portion of the SIM 1 and SIM 2 dataset in the tables that follow. The tables show the data entries to be populated for the ADN and SMS EFs. Each entry indicates the slot or record position in the EF to occupy, some key characteristics of the data entry, and the actual data contents, which correspond to that specified in the XML representation found in the data files.

Note that the tables list only those record positions to be populated with data; empty positions are not listed. The main languages involved are English (en), French (fr), and Japanese (ja). Miscellaneous accented characters from other languages also appear in the dataset. Extended (Ext.) characters refer to the 2-septet extensions to the GSM 7-bit alphabet (i.e., ^ { } \ [~] | and €). Null, zero-length record fields are possible and should not be confused with fields containing only one or more spaces. Other details can be determined from the XML data files in the SIMfill distribution package, which serve as the authoritative representation.

Slot	Text Length	Lang.	Special Char.	Ext. Char.		Type of Num.	Num. Length
2	short	en	Y			national	0
	0-digit number						
3	0					national	10
							3019758000
4	10	en	Y			national	10
	10-char en						3019758000
5	20	en	Y			national	10
	20-char entry paddin						3019758000
6	30	en	Y			national	10
	30-char entry pAaaaaaaaaaAdding						3019758000
7	40	en	Y			national	10
	40-char entry pAaaaaaaaaaAaaaaaaaaaadding						3019758000
8	50	en	Y			national	10
	50-char entry pAaaaaaaaaaAaaaaaaaaaaAaaaaaaaaadding						3019758000
9	100	en	Y			national	10
	100-char entry pAaaaaaaaaaAaaaaaaaaaaAaaaaaa…aadding						3019758000
10	275	en	Y			national	10
	275-char entry pAaaaaaaaaaAaaaaaaaaaaAaaaaaa…aadding						3019758000
12	1	space				national	10
							3019758000
13	1		Y			national	10
	@						3019758000
14	short	fr	Y			national	10
	En deÇà @ nist.gov						3019758000
15	short	en		Y		international	11
	English [ee] entry						13019758000
16	short	fr	Y			national	20
	Élément francais						01181337190123456789
17	short	en	Y			national	20+
	Extra data in EF_EXT1						30130197597580008000
19	short		Y			unknown	2
	@£$¥ !"#						17
20	short		Y			unknown	2
	¤%&'()*+,						27
21	short		Y			unknown	2
	-./:;<=>?						37
22	short	misc.	Y			unknown	2
	¡§¿èéùòÇ						47
23	short	misc.				unknown	2
	ØøÅåÆæßÉÄ						57
24	short	misc.				unknown	2
	ÖÑÜäöñüà						67
25	short			Y		unknown	2
	^{}\[~]|€						77

50

SIM1 – 7-bit GSM encoded SMS entries

Slot	Direction	Read/ Sent	Deleted	Old DST	New DST	Length	Msg. Part	Lang.	Special Char.	Ext. Char.	Picture
1	incoming	Y			Y	short		en			
1	0123456789ABCDEFGHIJKLMNOPQRSTUVWXYZabcdefghijklmnopqrstuvwxyz										
2	incoming		Y			short		fr			
2	Message court écrit en francais										
3	incoming					long	1/2	en	Y	Y	
3	Concatenated long English message part 1/2 }										
4	incoming					long	2/2	en	Y	Y	
4	{ Concatenated long English message part 2/2										
5	outgoing	Y				long	1/2	fr		Y	
5	Long message écrit en francais }										
6	incoming		Y			short		en	Y		large
6	()										
7	outgoing	Y				long	2/2	fr		Y	small
7	{ avec une image []										
8	incoming		Y			long	3/3	en	Y	Y	
8	{ Concatenated long English message part 3/3 with part 1 & 2 erased										
9	incoming	Y				0					
9											
10	outgoing					short		misc.	Y	Y	
10	@£$¥èéùìòÇØøÅå_^{}\[~]|€ÆæßÉ !"#¤%&'()*+,-./:;<=>?¡ÄÖÑÜ§¿äöñüà										

SIM2 – UCS2 encoded ADN entries

Slot	Text Length	Lang.	Special Char.	Ext. Char.	Type of Num.	Num. Length
2	short	en	Y		national	0
	0-digit number					
3	0				national	10
						3019758000
4	10	en	Y		national	10
	10-char en					3019758000
5	20	en	Y		national	10
	20-char entry paddin					3019758000
6	30	en	Y		national	10
	30-char entry pAaaaaaaaaAdding					3019758000
7	40	en	Y		national	10
	40-char entry pAaaaaaaaaaAaaaaaaaaaadding					3019758000
8	50	en	Y		national	10
	50-char entry pAaaaaaaaaaAaaaaaaaaaaAaaaaaaaadding					3019758000
9	100	en	Y		national	10
	100-char entry pAaaaaaaaaaAaaaaaaaaaaAaaaaaa…aadding					3019758000
10	120	en	Y		national	10
	120-char entry pAaaaaaaaaaAaaaaaaaaaaAaaaaaa…aadding					3019758000
12	1	space			national	10
						3019758000
13	1		Y		national	10
	@					3019758000
14	short	fr	Y		national	10
	En deÇà @ nist.gov					3019758000
15	short	en		Y	international	11
	English [ee] entry					13019758000
16	short	ja	Y		national	20
	宮本 武蔵					01181337190123456789
17	short	en	Y		national	20+
	Extra data in EF_EXT1					30130197597580008000
19	short		Y		unknown	2
	@£$¥ !"#					17
20	short		Y		unknown	2
	¤%&'()*+,					27
21	short		Y		unknown	2
	-./:;<=>?					37
22	short	misc.	Y		unknown	2
	¡§¿èéùòÇ					47
23	short	misc.	Y		unknown	2
	ØøÅåÆæßÉÄ					57
24	short	misc.	Y		unknown	2
	ÖÑÜäöñüà					67
25	short			Y	unknown	2
	^{}\[~]|€					77

SIM2 – UCS2 encoded SMS entries

Slot	Direction	Read/Sent	Deleted	Old DST	New DST	Length	Msg. Part	Lang.	Special Char.	Ext. Char.	Picture
1	incoming	Y			Y	short		en			
	0123456789ABCDEFGHIJKLMNOPQRSTUVWXYZabcdefghijklmnopqrstuvwxyz										
2	incoming		Y			short		ja			
	これは長いメッセージです。										
3	incoming					long	1/2	en	Y	Y	
	Concatenated long English message part 1/2 }										
4	incoming					long	2/2	en	Y	Y	
	{ Concatenated long English message part 2/2										
5	outgoing	Y				long	1/2	ja		Y	
	これは長いメッセージです。 }										
6	incoming			Y		short		en	Y		large
	()										
7	outgoing	Y				long	2/2	ja		Y	small
	{ これは長いメッセージです。 []										
8	incoming		Y			long	3/3	en	Y	Y	
	{ Concatenated long English message part 3/3 with part 1 & 2 erased										
9	incoming	Y				0					
11	outgoing					short		misc.	Y	Y	
	@£$¥èéùìòÇØøÅå_^{}\[~]|€ÆæßÉ !"#¤%&'()*+,-./:;<=>?¡ÄÖÑÜ§¿äöñüà										